Live an
INSPIRING
Life

Live an
INSPIRING
Life

10 Secret Ingredients for Inner Strength

Wally Amos
with Stu Glauberman

Blue Mountain Press ®

Boulder, Colorado

Library of Congress Catalog Card Number: 2006007785
ISBN-13: 978-1-59842-167-5
ISBN-10: 1-59842-167-0

Certain trademarks are used under license.
BLUE MOUNTAIN PRESS is registered in U.S. Patent and Trademark Office.

Printed in the United States of America.
First Printing: 2006

 This book is printed on recycled paper.

This book is printed on fine quality, laid embossed, 80 lb. paper. This paper has been specially produced to be acid free (neutral pH) and contains no groundwood or unbleached pulp. It conforms with all the requirements of the American National Standards Institute, Inc., so as to ensure that this book will last and be enjoyed by future generations.

Library of Congress Cataloging-in-Publication Data

Amos, Wally.
Live an inspiring life : 10 secret ingredients for inner strength / Wally Amos and Stu Glauberman.
     p. cm.
   ISBN 1-59842-167-0 (trade pbk. : alk. paper) 1. Success. 2. Conduct of life. 3. Inspiration. I. Glauberman, Stu.
II. Title.

BJ1611.2.A47 2006
158'.1--dc22

                                                                            2006007785

Blue Mountain Arts, Inc.

P.O. Box 4549, Boulder, Colorado 80306

CONTENTS

Introduction 7

Love 9

Positive Attitude 15

Self-Esteem 21

Commitment 25

Integrity 31

Giving 37

Imagination 43

Enthusiasm 49

Words 53

Faith 59

Conclusion 63

About Wally Amos 64

INTRODUCTION

WHENEVER I bake cookies, I choose the best ingredients I can find. As someone who takes pride in what I make or bake, I never compromise on ingredients. When I share my thoughts on what I do to live a happy, fulfilling, inspiring life, I also begin with the best ingredients. In my first book, *The Power in You*, written with my son Gregory over fifteen years ago, I identified ten items that were essential to my recipe for inner strength. So much has happened to me since then, and I am continually amazed that I still rely on those same items for inner strength. As I share them, you'll see there's really nothing secret about these ingredients. The only secret is that they are always there, always at hand, always ready to be combined, mixed, and stirred into the batter to make our lives better.

Before we begin, rummage around in the cupboard of your soul in search of these ingredients:

LOVE	GIVING
POSITIVE ATTITUDE	IMAGINATION
SELF-ESTEEM	ENTHUSIASM
COMMITMENT	WORDS
INTEGRITY	FAITH

Keep these ten ingredients handy at all times. No substitutions, please. Individually, they are just ingredients, but combine them together and you will create something extraordinary: a stronger, happier, more inspiring, and joyful you.

LOVE

WHATEVER THE QUESTION, LOVE IS THE ANSWER.

Love is the most powerful force in the universe. To live an inspiring life, you must keep love in mind, hold love in your heart, and add love to everything you make.

EVERYONE wants to be loved, and if you're like a lot of people, you're laboring under a well-defined misconception of what love is, how you want to be loved, and by whom you want to be loved. I've met people who keep a mental laundry list of the qualities they expect from the person they want to fall in love with and be loved by. It's no wonder some people describe themselves as unlucky in love. We're all familiar with the poet's lament, "'Tis better to have loved and lost than never to have loved at all." I, for one, don't believe that you can love and lose. I believe that when you see there is something good, something to be loved, in every person, you will love and your love will be accepted and returned. That's always a win-win situation.

When I first envisioned my life as a cookie man, I decided right off the "batter" that my standard for success would not be how many cookies I made or how rich or famous I became. I set out to measure my success in love. That way, if my business plans failed and my cookie company went under or I went broke, I would still be whole. Money comes and goes, and if fame finds you, it is usually as fleeting as the hangers-on who linger around celebrities for their own gain. But if you identify love as the most important thing in your life, you will always have something to give you strength.

Learning to love can be the secret of your success in life. It's never too late to reexamine your beliefs and values, make changes, and let love into your life. To attain the level of love I'm talking about, you must apply love to everything you think, do, and say. Becoming a totally loving person is not easy, but with practice, your every thought can be a thought of love and every action the action of a loving person. When I think of this ideal, I am reminded of a line in Victor Hugo's *Les Miserables*: "To love another person is to see the face of God."

To be someone who loves and is loved by others, you must first love yourself. Do you think of yourself as unlovable? Do you believe there is something about you that keeps others from loving you? If you think there is some kind of love repellent that keeps people from being attracted to you, you're right. The repellent is your judgments about yourself and your failure to forgive yourself. The only way to get rid of it is to love yourself for all that you are.

And to achieve the kind of love that inspires others and brings many returns, you must love unconditionally, expecting nothing in return. When I say love is blind, I'm not talking about falling in love with someone who doesn't match your laundry list of suitors. The love I'm describing is blind because it does not discriminate against race, color, sex, creed, religion, height, or weight. It is nonjudgmental. It is impossible to love someone if you stand in judgment of what that person does or says. Let your judgments go. Let your fears go. Respond with love.

If you're a Beatles fan, you know the Fab Four morphed from mop tops to mystics and from rockers to revolutionaries. Through all the experimental lifestyles and radical politics, and from their impoverished roots to their remarkable financial success, they never abandoned the notion "all you need is love" and its corollary, "love is all there is." It's interesting to note that the first hits penned by John Lennon and Paul McCartney were "Love Me Do" and "P.S., I Love You," and a decade later, in the last line of the last song the Beatles ever recorded, "The End," their parting words were, "And in the end, the love you take is equal to the love you make."

I was never good at math. I could never figure out what X was or why. But I am a true believer and devotee of the mysterious calculus of love: that the more love you give away, the more you have.

I believed for many years that I was not good at being loved. I attributed the failure of my first two marriages to the idea that I had never experienced love and did not know how to share myself with others. Over the years, I've come to understand that I was immature when it came to relationships. No matter what your chronological age, you are not mature enough to maintain a relationship unless you put the needs of your loved one ahead of your own.

Real love is unconditional love. To give unconditional love, you must learn to love others for who they are, not what they do. It's not easy to become a person who can love naturally and unconditionally. It can take a long time — hopefully not a lifetime — to learn how to love. But if you don't make an effort to love yourself for who you are and love others for who they are, you rob yourself of the joy of loving effortlessly. The first step to opening your heart is to open your mind. Once you accept that your perspective is not the only viewpoint, you begin to see more of what the world, and everyone in it, has to offer.

It is impossible to love others if you are eager to judge and unwilling to accept what you see in them. The same is true about loving yourself, which is the prerequisite to loving someone else. You invite love when you stand free of the screen that makes it easier to judge than be judged.

1 Corinthians 13:4-7 tells us, "Love is patient and kind. Love is not jealous or boastful or proud or rude. Love does not demand its own way. Love is not irritable, and it keeps no record of when it has been wronged. It is never glad about injustice but rejoices whenever the truth wins out. Love never gives up, never loses faith, is always hopeful, and endures through every circumstance."

Secret Ingredient: LOVE
Begin with a full measure of self-respect. Add equal measures of patience, compassion, and understanding. Mix well, being careful not to add conditions of any kind.

FINAL WORDS:

To love another person is to help them love God.
— *Søren Kierkegaard*

Love is the answer to all questions.
— *Wally Amos*

POSITIVE ATTITUDE

I am upset not by events but rather by the way I view them.
— *Epictetus, first century AD*

MANY PEOPLE tell me it's easy for me to be positive about life because I'm famous. What they fail to understand is that I'm famous because I've developed a positive mental attitude, which in turn has created a positive life. The advantage of a positive attitude is that it tells you life is never really what it appears to be — it is always more.

I wasn't always so positive. For years I wanted what I didn't have and blamed everyone else for my not having it. All of this required an abundance of negativity, and negativity feeds on itself.

What I learned over time, after many unfortunate, self-inflicted experiences, is that you can actually choose your feelings, your behavior, and your attitude. You can choose the results in your life. In every situation you encounter, you have a choice. You can always choose the positive.

Perhaps you or someone you know is like I was: I didn't know what I wanted to do, only what I didn't want to do and where, when, how, and with whom I didn't want to do it. How negative can you get? Finally, in the early seventies, I found what I needed to help me live a more fulfilled life. And, of course, I found it where you always find something that's been missing: in the last place you think to look. I found that what I needed was inside me all the time. And what was it? A new attitude!

Awareness is the first condition for creating your world as you want it to be. Begin by unlearning everything you thought was going to bring you happiness. Accept the present and let go of the past. When we live in the present, we live a longer, happier, and more useful life.

Now here's a real secret: you can create the circumstances you want in your life right now by developing a positive mental attitude. This alone will create a positive environment around you, because your attitude creates your reality. A positive mental attitude not only helps you visualize what you want to be, it helps you become it.

Okay, you say, it's easy to have a positive attitude when the cookies turn out perfect every time you bake, everyone knows you because you have "Famous" before your name, and you have money in the bank (or you're at least current on your credit card balance). It's not so easy to maintain a positive attitude if you're down and out, you say. I've learned the hard way that a famous name and money in the bank are not true measures of happiness. Far more valuable than fame and fortune are good health and peace of mind.

Even when your health fails, you can cultivate peace of mind. How many people do you know who are suffering from life-threatening or life-changing, crippling illnesses? As I travel around the country, I am amazed at how many people I meet who have been afflicted by some physical disorder, yet they manage to carry on mentally and spiritually with the positive attitudes of people who have been blessed.

Peggy Chun, a well-known watercolor artist in Hawaii, has been beset by ALS (Lou Gehrig's disease). Almost four years ago, she lost movement in her right hand and took to painting with her left hand. When she lost movement in her left hand, she began painting by holding the brush in her teeth. When she could no longer move her head, she instructed her friends on how to move her head for her, creating what she calls "eye-paintings." With her sharp mind, eyesight, and hearing intact, she refuses to quit, saying "I am living with ALS, not dying from ALS."

If you're healthy enough to pace the floor and flail your arms around over nagging doubts and negativism, look to those who are debilitated by real ailments and physical pain. If they can still manage to be positive, so can you. Follow their lead.

Do you ever blame your misfortunes on bad luck? Bad luck is a state of mind. If you believe you have it, you do. The same is true for good luck. Good luck doesn't just happen to you. You make it happen. Choose to believe that the universe is a friendly place. If you shine the light of a positive attitude into the mist of new ideas, you will create good-luck rainbows in your mind. It's up to you to keep superstition and the black cats of despair from crossing your path.

You can actually visualize a good outcome for yourself. The chief executive officer of a company based in Honolulu was forced to take his company into Chapter 11 bankruptcy and lead thousands of employees through some really tough times. A year later, when the company emerged under very favorable conditions, the CEO was asked how he had kept such an optimistic outlook even when so many forces were at work trying to shut the company down. He said that on the very first day he filed for bankruptcy protection, he had visualized the moment when he would stand up in a courtroom to thank the judge, the company's employees, and its business partners for securing a successful outcome. And it came to pass.

We all have our daily challenges and disappointments. What has worked exceptionally well for me is that I have been able to create a cheerful world for myself. Whether you're happy or miserable depends more on your attitude than your circumstance. This is not a new idea. Martha Washington articulated it more than two hundred years ago: "I am determined to be cheerful and happy in whatever situation I may find myself. For I have learned that the greater part of our misery or unhappiness is determined not by our circumstance but by our disposition." Additionally, it was Abraham Lincoln who said, "People are about as happy as they make up their minds to be."

This is a lesson that I, too, have learned. You choose to call yourself happy or unhappy. You are the writer, producer, editor, and director of your life story. If you write the script correctly, you will be the star and the hero of your production. Once you picture yourself as a happy person with a positive outlook, others will see you that way, too, and they will want to be like you.

Be happy and have fun. Choose to enjoy every day.

Secret Ingredient: POSITIVE ATTITUDE
Begin by being your best today. Use only the freshest ideas of what you can accomplish and discard all the thoughts that are past their expiration dates. Keep your mind on the things you want and off the things you do not want. Focus on answers and solutions.

FINAL WORDS:

Human beings, by changing the inner attitudes of their minds, can change the outer aspects of their lives.
— *William James*

When you change your attitude, you can change your life.
— *Jerry Jampolsky and Diane Cirincione*

SELF-ESTEEM

We are to ourselves just what we think we are.
— *Phineas Parkhurst Quimby*

HAD I KNOWN the term, I could have been the poster boy for
the affliction known as an Inferiority Complex. I arrived up north
from Tallahassee, Florida, as a twelve-year-old thinking I was a
no-count fellow with no chance of getting ahead. Years later, when
I entered the job market in New York City, I was still thinking pretty
much the same thing. I spent twenty years letting people tell me
I wasn't good enough for this or that. How low can you go? That's
where I was, but as they say, "I've come a long way, Baby!"

For years, I've written and lectured extensively on self-esteem.
I've got to say that it's one of my favorite things to talk about
because it's such an essential ingredient in developing inner
strength and living a healthy, happy, and inspiring life.

When we're not sure of ourselves and we don't stop to think for
ourselves, we allow others to frame our self-image. As a teenager
new to New York City, I constantly compared myself to the junior
high school hip kids and found myself lacking for one imagined
reason or another. I was my own worst enemy. The simple truth
is: you cannot be a failure without your own consent. Only
through self-examination can you begin to build self-esteem. As
in baking cookies, you need ingredients to build self-confidence.
In the case of self-image, begin by taking inventory of yourself.

Forget what you think you lack and remind yourself of all that you have to offer.

A first step is to realize that you are unique, an individual expression of God, and a priceless, irreplaceable work of art. You are truly a one-of-a-kind collector's item. The "auction" value you place on yourself is entirely up to you. No one will raise the stakes on your future if you don't start the bidding.

With that in mind, continue to identify your own unique characteristics. There might be some things about yourself that you choose to change, but you cannot change them until you identify them. Each day, work on finding new things about yourself — the diamonds that you treasure and the gravel that you want to leave outside. Write them down and continue to affirm them.

You have the free will and the choice to take full responsibility for your self-image. Stop being your own worst enemy and be your own best friend. There's only one person who can lift up your low self-esteem and raise it to the heights of self-love and self-confidence, and that's you. Treat yourself with love and respect. You will spend every day of your life with yourself, so start appreciating the great person that you are today!

The eyes you use to look upon yourself in the mirror every morning are the same eyes you use to take in the magnificence of nature, the patent beauty of models and movie stars, and the heartwarming magic of a smile. Imagine your eyes as fountains spilling outward. If you project your unique viewpoint from the inside out, the world becomes what you want to see and a reflection of who you are within. People will see you as you wish them to see you. Your view of the world depends on how you look on yourself. If you look at it that way, the whole world is waiting for you to hold yourself in high regard so it can, too. Life is an inside job!

Secret Ingredient: SELF-ESTEEM
Remember you choose how you see yourself. Start with acceptance of and compassion for your finer qualities, and fold these into something you can knead. Work on it until smooth.

FINAL WORDS:

The soul that is within me no man can degrade.
— *Frederick Douglass*

COMMITMENT

To commit or procrastinate? That is the question.

THE LARGEST obstacle between you and your goal is your lack of total commitment. Quit saying "if only" and "I wish it were that easy." Rid yourself of these thoughts and adopt the attitude that it is as easy as you make it.

When most people hear the word "commitment," they think of people who are teeter-tottering and trying to decide whether marriage or living together is the right move. True enough, there can be no true love relationship without true commitment. I know, because I entered into several relationships with the half-baked notion that I could do just so much in the way of commitment and shirk doing the rest.

Women who are searching for the perfect man often wonder how they will know that a suitor is really suitable. It's the age-old question set forth in "The Shoop Shoop Song (It's in His Kiss)": *How can I tell if he loves me so? Is it in his eyes... his face... or his warm embrace?* The songwriter concludes, "It's in his kiss." Suppose he has talented lips but lacks commitment. Which would you choose — a suitor with hot lips or a suitor with a strong sense of commitment? Why not test the ardor of the person whose arms you want to hold you? Ask him to put those loving arms to good use doing your laundry. In fact, this will test you both. Do you trust him with your things? Will he agree to do it if you ask him? Will he do a good job? There's more to a relationship than kissing. Is he interested in being a playmate or a helpmate?

In the novel *Captain Corelli's Mandolin*, author Louis de Bernières describes the difference between romantic love and abiding love through the voice of a philosophical Greek father having a conversation with his lovelorn daughter: "Love is a temporary madness, it erupts like volcanoes and then subsides," the father counsels. While any fool can be in love, true love, he advises, is "what is left over when being in love has burned away." Love, itself, is like two roots growing together and becoming entwined for all purposes.

In a real love relationship, commitment is the magnetism that keeps two people together and makes their mutual happiness possible. Being committed to a person, an ideal, or a way of life isn't easy. It requires effort. Commitment forces you to keep everything in perspective and to keep everything current. You can't fall behind in your commitment and pay it back later.

If you're committed to someone or something, show you're committed today and don't wait until tomorrow. Today is worth two tomorrows. Don't use excuses like, "I might," "I really should," and "I ought to." Use the words "I will" and you will see that commitment leads to action, and one action leads to another, which sets off a chain reaction. Commitment brings the satisfaction and fun of getting things done. It can make dreams come true.

I love reading, and I love to promote reading by reading aloud to children and their parents. I even read children's books during my lectures. One of the most enduring children's books is *The Little Engine That Could*. It's about a train that has to get over a mountain. The little train discovers the strength to climb the imposing mountain through the practice of positive thought, expressed in the very powerful refrain, "I think I can. I think I can." As a child, I was a self-doubter. Mired in low self-esteem, I was the "kid who couldn't," because I thought I couldn't. I used the words "I can't" as an excuse to prevent myself from making the initial effort to do anything I thought I couldn't do. If I had learned the lesson of the determined little train engine, I might have discovered my inner strength much earlier in my life. When I was thirty-nine and detractors scoffed at the idea that the Famous Amos Chocolate-Chip Cookie could succeed as a stand-alone shop on Hollywood's Sunset Boulevard, I became the Little Cookie-Maker That Could. From the self-esteem I gained as the Little Cookie-Maker That Could — and Did! — I became the Big Cookie-Maker Who Could — all because I had learned to trust myself.

Commitment is what separates the achievers from the should-haves and would-haves and might-haves. Never mind that people say it can't be done and that others have failed at it. Focus on the idea that you may be the one chosen to do it. Making a commitment in a romantic relationship or a business relationship is like throwing a stone into still water: the initial action sends out ripples that carry positive impulses forward.

When I was discharged from the Air Force in 1957, I went back to New York City, not knowing what I would do or what I was capable of doing. I wound up using the G.I. Bill to enroll in a secretarial school. Both the owner of the school and her sister, who became my mentor, made a commitment from the start to see me through, and this in turn emboldened me to commit myself to stay the course. Their enthusiastic commitment to my success led to my own commitment, enthusiasm, and confidence. As a result, I have learned that the best way to encourage commitment from someone is to place your trust in that person.

The poet, novelist, and dramatist Johann Wolfgang von Goethe suggested that all acts of creation stem from the moment of deciding to commit oneself to an initiative. He observed, "A whole stream of events issues from the decision, raising in one's favor all manner of unforeseen incidents, meetings, and material assistance, which no man could have dreamt would have come his way." In other words, if you get the ball rolling, the universe will help it pick up speed.

How many times have you told yourself, "I'll get around to it when the time is right"? The best time to start anything worth doing is when you get the idea. The degree to which you will succeed depends on your commitment to that idea. Goethe also wrote, "Boldness has genius, power and magic in it. Only engage (yourself), and the mind grows heated. Begin it and the work will be completed."

It's much simpler when you put it this way: If you don't start, you can't finish. Do it now!

Secret Ingredient: COMMITMENT

Lay out all your doubts and maybes on the table. Now scrape them off and replace them with positive thinking to the effect that you can finish what you start.

FINAL WORDS:

Commitment is the match that lights the fire.
— *Wally Amos*

INTEGRITY

*Let there be a new high standard of honesty, industry, and
integrity in our society, and let it begin with me.*

IF YOU do not stand for something, you will fall for anything.
Morality, integrity, and ethics are the building blocks for the kind
of inner strength that becomes the foundation of a successful life
and a progressive society.

You may think that integrity and ethics are handed down from
government and drilled into us by religious and educational
institutions. I believe that these important ingredients for inner
strength, like every important ingredient in life, spring from the
individual. Integrity begins with the individual and radiates into
the institutions and communities we create. Integrity must be
internal. Others cannot impose it on us.

To have integrity is to be honest, beginning with yourself and
those closest to you. As a brash, selfish young man embarking on
a career as a talent agent, I was not honest with myself or those
who loved me. Reflecting on that time in my life, I realize that I
was attempting to fool others and even myself. In my first two
marriages, I managed to split myself into two different people
operating in two different worlds. One world was filled with lies
and the other was filled with half-truths. Once you start cranking
out lies, it's difficult to remember what you said. The satirist Mark
Twain noted that if you tell the truth, you don't have to remember
as much. I suppose some of my lies were crafted to make my

wife feel better at the time. The result of all the lies I heaped high atop each other was that I made myself, and everyone around me, miserable. Peace of mind is only possible when you tell the truth.

When I outgrew the game, stopped being a player, and started being a responsible and caring person, I scraped up all the integrity I could muster and became truthful. I began by being honest with myself. Then I extended that truthfulness to those who knew me and those who entered my life. It's not easy to make a 180-degree turn in your personality. It takes time and patience. But it's worth doing. Shakespeare's Polonius counseled Laertes in *Hamlet,* "This above all: to thine ownself be true." This is probably the best advice an adult can give a child after "be careful crossing the street." If you're honest with yourself, you will know what to do when you come to every corner and prepare to cross every street. You will have a reservoir of integrity to draw upon in every part of your life — both in personal and professional relationships. Whenever and wherever you come into contact with other people, integrity and ethics will show you the way.

Buddhists say that if the mind becomes impure, one's deeds will become impure and the result will be suffering. The best way to prevent suffering is to keep the mind pure and honest.

We are all familiar with what happens to people in the public eye when they lose their way and are shown to be crooks, liars, or welshers. They are pilloried in the media and left without a shred of dignity. And the public seems to demand that the bigger they are, the harder they should fall. Ralph Waldo Emerson spoke of "the sacredness of private integrity." I can think of few things more sacred than keeping yourself honest and whole in private and in public. Build up your inner strength by developing the muscle of integrity within you.

Not long ago, the passing of a woman named Rosa Parks reminded the nation how one person's integrity can inspire others and lead to fundamental social changes. Riding home from work on a city bus in Montgomery, Alabama in 1955, the dignified black seamstress defied the Jim Crow laws that made blacks second-class citizens. She simply refused to give up her seat for a white man. In her book, *My Story*, Rosa Parks says it wasn't that she was tired after a day of work; she was just fed up with the injustice of segregation laws. "No," she wrote, "the only tired I was, was tired of giving in." She was found guilty and fined ten dollars, but her act of defiance inspired a boycott of the city bus system by blacks — and eventually a U.S. Supreme Court ruling barring segregation on public buses — and thus she became an icon of the modern civil rights movement. In his book, *Strive for Freedom*, Dr. Martin Luther King, Jr. called Rosa Parks' decision "an individual expression of a timeless longing for human dignity and freedom." Her strength to sit down and fight came from knowing she was right and the law was wrong. "She was planted there by her personal sense of dignity and self-respect," wrote Dr. King. "She was anchored to that seat by the accumulated indignities of days gone and the boundless aspirations of generations yet unborn." In 1996, President Clinton awarded Rosa Parks the Presidential Medal of Freedom, the highest honor the nation bestows upon civilians. Upon her death in October 2005, Reverend Jesse Jackson said: "She sat down in order that we might stand up."

My mother, Ruby, was a devout churchgoer who believed in the right and wrong and the good and bad of the Bible. She was a strict disciplinarian who drew a lot of lines and gave me "a lickin'" when I stepped over any of them. If I did something bad, I got a beating for my own good. Disciplinarians and schoolteachers of the "old school" have argued that the way to learn what's right is to have it beaten into you. I believe there are more enlightened ways to learn, and one of them is to learn by example.

One day in 1944, more than a decade before Rosa Parks refused to give up her seat, Ruby and I were on our way back from church when we found ourselves in a similar situation on a Tallahassee bus. As in Montgomery, the front of the bus was reserved for whites and the back for blacks. The only rider up front on this Sunday morning was the bus driver's girlfriend. When Ruby chose to sit down in front, the girlfriend complained to the driver, who told us to move to the back of the bus. "I paid my money and I'm gonna sit where I please," Ruby said. Faced with Ruby's refusal to budge, the driver stopped at a bus depot seeking help in dealing with this uppity so-and-so. I was frightened, but Ruby was resolute. The driver came back alone, weighed his options, and chose to do nothing. Ruby rejoiced in her small victory. I was impressed with her courage and conviction that she was right and that segregation laws were wrong. On that day I saw for myself that my mother was indeed a woman of integrity.

Closely entwined with integrity is morality, which deals with what's good and right and how to behave well and honestly. Misfortune begins in the mind. What you choose to believe is up to you. Whatever religion or spiritual path you follow, it will guide you to right-thinking. Then it is up to you to steer your behavior toward what is right. If a teaching is heartfelt, put your heart into it and live it. The fastest way out of a bad situation may not be the right way out. The right way out is the best way out. Doing the right thing brings the right reward. If you do it right the first time, it's less likely you'll have to do it again.

Secret Ingredient: INTEGRITY
Reach inside yourself to find this ingredient. Do not let yourself be fooled by insincere imitations of yourself. Stick to the quality brand, which is the truth.

FINAL WORDS:

Who you are speaks so loudly
I can't hear what you are saying.
— *Ralph Waldo Emerson*

GIVING

To give and to receive are in truth one and the same.

SOME PEOPLE see life as a straight line and imagine that all humanity is passing through in single file, trying to get to the head of the line by hook or by crook. I have discovered that if you lead a life of giving, you see life as a circle with everyone holding hands. What you give as part of a circle comes back to you. When you give love and peace, you get love and peace. When you give hate, you get hate. When you give to the enormous circle that is the world, your gift multiplies and has an effect not only on the individuals directly involved, but on all humankind.

What's your definition of charity? The author Jack London, who loved to write about dogs, said that giving a bone to a dog is not charity. "Charity," he said, "is the bone shared with the dog, when you are just as hungry as the dog." Reverend Frederick Eikerenkoetter (better known as Reverend Ike) once said, "Giving someone in need of shoes a pair from your closet full of shoes is not giving. Giving someone your last pair of shoes is giving your shoes." It's often said that charity begins at home. Many people interpret this to mean that you shouldn't be focused on giving to the needy in some far-off place when there are needy people in your own neighborhood. I take this to mean that charity begins in your home, in your heart, and in every aspect of life. If charity begins at home, it should not remain at home. It should get out and about. I personally have a spiritual belief that says everything in my life comes through me, not from me. It comes from an infinite Higher Source. I call this source God, but it has many names, and the name is not important. When I connect with that Higher Source, I know that I am not the giver; I am just a channel.

On the day after Christmas in 2004, a powerful earthquake in Sumatra at the northern tip of Indonesia triggered a killer tidal wave that tore across the Indian Ocean, causing death and devastation in Indonesia and Asia. The destruction was described as "beyond belief." So was the outpouring of giving that followed in the first weeks and months of 2005. It began with the big nations and major international organizations, but it rippled throughout the world: through cities, large and small, and on down to schoolchildren, who collected pennies that became tens of thousands of dollars. Americans were surprised to see two political enemies, the former presidents George Herbert Walker Bush and Bill Clinton, join together to appeal for cash donations to aid the tsunami victims. Their unified message about giving from the heart was simple: "No one can change what happened," said Bush. "But we can all change what happens next," said Clinton.

What is your definition of giving? Is it limited to donating money and material goods to the needy? A great part of our lives is concerned with getting money, status, and things. Eventually, there comes a time when we begin to see that we can also give spiritually. When I think back on all the things I've done, the most meaningful experiences in my life were not about getting money for myself, but about giving of myself to help others. There is a wealth of contentment that comes from giving of oneself.

I believe that if you lead a life of service to your fellow human beings and give your all to that purpose, you can free yourself from the negative influence of worrying. Take it from someone who's been rich and famous *and* on the verge of bankruptcy: there is no value to fortune or fame unless it can be used to help others. Celebrity is nothing more than being known by those who do not know you. It carries no value.

If your mailbox is like mine, it is filled each day by letters from charitable organizations seeking donations. The reason so many charities are forced to solicit funds through the mail is that there are so many people with needs that aren't being met. I like to think of charitable causes as vehicles for giving. They are a means that allows us to open our hearts along with our wallets. The act of giving and serving is one that pays a double dividend by doing good and making you feel good.

Of course, there are many ways to give without giving money. Giving can be of your time, your hands, and your heart. Most of the people we recognize as heroes do not wake up saying, "I will be a hero today." Rather, they find themselves in a situation where help is needed and jump in, not expecting any reward other than the satisfaction of helping another human being. You don't have to be a hero to be a helper. Reverend Sam Heinz said it better than anyone I've heard yet: "The only reason we exist is to serve each other."

I believe that part of our responsibility as human beings is to find ways to give. Many years ago, back when I had my Famous Amos store in Hollywood, I linked the activity of making cookies with the activity of improving reading skills. These activities may seem unrelated to you, but not to me, simply because I love making cookies and I love encouraging people to read.

I saw for myself at Holly Park Library in Hawthorne, California, how excited children could get over reading books. I challenged them to read eight books over a two-week period, and I rewarded those who did with a one-pound bag of cookies. Over a three-month period I gave away fifteen hundred pounds of cookies, but I took great satisfaction looking at those young readers and knowing that cookies would sweeten their lives in one way, but reading would sweeten their lives in many ways.

Making cookies has been both a livelihood and a way of life for me. Encouraging children to read, being the spokesman for Literacy Volunteers of America, and promoting my Read It Loud! campaigns have been both commitments and joys. It's having vehicles for giving that are really fun for me. In my latest cookie business, a little store called Chip & Cookie in my hometown of Kailua, Hawaii, on Oahu, I have added a reading corner fully stocked with books where parents come and read to their children. When I'm at the store I can enjoy selling cookies and reading aloud. Cookies and reading: food for the tummy, food for thought, and feel-good food for the soul.

What you take from others is how you make your living. What you give to others is how you live your life. Giving begets giving.

Secret Ingredient: GIVING

Like love, this ingredient is difficult to measure. The more you pour out, the more you get back.

FINAL WORDS:

Charity is never lost. It may meet with ingratitude, or be of no service to those on whom it was bestowed, yet it ever does a work of beauty and grace upon the heart of the giver.

— *Conyers Middleton*

IMAGINATION

*The real voyage of discovery consists not in exploring
new landscapes but in having new eyes.*

EINSTEIN SAID that imagination was more important than
knowledge. I can't imagine arguing with Einstein! It was the
philosophical Spanish painter and sculptor Pablo Picasso who put
forth the idea that everything you can imagine is real. Of course,
you don't need to be an artist to paint a mental picture. Just use
the paintbox that is your imagination. Imagine for a moment that
you are in paradise. What does it look like? How does it feel to be
there? What does it sound like, smell like? What is there to eat?
Can you taste it? That paradise may not be a real place, but it's
real to you if you can see it and feel it and taste it.

Whatever you intend to achieve must first be imagined. Visualizing
what you want makes it possible. However, first you have to invest
yourself in the vision. You've got to love whatever it is that you
want before you can love what you're going to have to do to get it.
In his hit song "I Believe I Can Fly," singer-songwriter R. Kelly says:
"If I can see it, then I can do it. If I believe it, there's nothing to
it." This matches my credo precisely. I used to bake chocolate-chip
cookies and give them to Hollywood celebrities who really ate them
up. I began to imagine what might happen if I opened a store on
Hollywood's Sunset Strip that sold homemade-style chocolate-chip
cookies? What if I became famous as an entrepreneur of cookies?
What if I organized a marching band of kazoo players to promote

the Famous Amos Chocolate-Chip Cookie Corporation? I thought about this until I believed it and could see it clearly, and then I did it and *everyone* could see it.

Human beings spend a lifetime seeking security. If you define security by what is secure, safe, and unthreatening to you and to what you know and are used to and comforted by, you are limiting your potential for new experiences, opportunities, growth, and emotions. Your sense of security should not rest on familiarity or what you have amassed in designer-label goods and material comfort, but rather on what you can achieve with your mind.

Imagination is one of the ingredients of an inspired life. You may never discover or create something entirely new. Still, you can see things with new eyes, add new interpretations, and bring new life to old ideas. Begin by looking for new ways to do things you've being doing the same way for years. Stretch your mind.

Some people say they are not creative. There are, in fact, individuals who are not curious by nature, who seldom, if ever, question what they are told or wonder about what they see. I believe that being incurious limits the ability to be creative. However, as long as you live, there will always be opportunities to open your eyes and ears and taste new things. If you take the time to examine life with all your senses, you will enliven your imagination and your horizons will expand.

You don't have to be an Einstein or an inventor to be imaginative. Everyone has imagination. You take yours for granted a thousand times a day. Like most people, you're probably faced with chores and responsibilities that are part of your daily routine. But your mind is at work the whole time, instructing you how to tackle the task immediately at hand, the business of the day, and the week ahead. Your imagination is giving hints as to how to express yourself in all that you do. Put your imagination to work for you like a lever that can lighten the heavy lifting of the day. Find ways to make every task more interesting. Imagine what lies ahead for you. Express yourself by doing things differently. Show the world how unique you are.

If you're not using your imagination, you're inviting yourself to stagnate and get stuck in a rut. You can choose to spend your day being mindful or mindless. Imagination will make the difference.

Life is an adventure. If you choose to, you can scale the highest peaks, jump out of airplanes, and spelunk or scuba dive to the depths of earth and sea. You can use your imagination to run wild. Imagine yourself an adventurer in life and make it happen.

Can you imagine a better world? The former Beatle John Lennon was on a crusade for world peace when he penned the words to his song "Imagine." A self-confessed dreamer, Lennon challenged his generation to imagine a world without the regional and religious differences that divide people and without the pursuit of personal wealth and material possessions. His 1971 lyrics imagined that by abandoning the institutions that separate us, we would all live together in peace, free of hunger and greed. Sound radical? Every religion and belief system I know of strives for peace on earth and goodwill to men. Can you imagine all of the world's people living their lives in peace? Can you imagine a way to achieve it?

Stretch your imagination. Think of something you can do today to make the world a better place.

Secret Ingredient: IMAGINATION

Imagination cannot be found on the same shelf as your everyday thoughts and habits. Search for it in new opportunities and in all the things you've always wanted to do that are fun to do and worth doing.

FINAL WORDS:

Go confidently in the direction of your dreams!
Live the life you have imagined.
— *Henry David Thoreau*

You see things; and you say, "Why?" But I dream things
that never were; and I say, "Why not?"
— *George Bernard Shaw*

Cautious people live longer but they never really live.
— *Author Unknown*

ENTHUSIASM

Age may wrinkle the face,
but lack of enthusiasm wrinkles the soul.

DO YOU count enthusiasm among the most important things in life? You should.

I've already mentioned a positive attitude as one of the key ingredients for inner strength. If you can achieve and maintain a positive mental attitude, you are on the right path to a satisfying life, but if you add enthusiasm to your daily routine, you will find yourself skipping merrily down that path.

A positive mental attitude provides the best environment for the body to heal. Enthusiasm is the lifeblood, the energy, and the moxie that makes it that much easier to mobilize and put knowledge and imagination into action. Enthusiasm powers your life like electricity powers a light bulb. Nothing happens to a light bulb until you flip the switch and release a surge of energy to illuminate it. In life, you are the light bulb, capable of glowing, but not until the enthusiasm is switched on.

The word "enthusiasm" is derived from the Greek words for "possessed" and "inspired." The root word is "enthos," which literally means the breath of God. Originally it had a negative connotation and was applied to a fanatic who was possessed by a false god or false belief. Today, we talk about enthusiasm as a positive ingredient in an inspiring life. Enthusiasm is what excites us, and I say, bring it on. The more enthusiastic you are, the more you are capable of inspiring enthusiasm in others.

Enthusiasm can win where antagonism loses. Let your thoughts and words be constructive, supportive, and loving, and your enthusiasm can defeat pessimism and turn frowns into smiles. Enthusiasm is the antidote to dull, lifeless lectures and presentations. What's more, enthusiasm is contagious. I remember reading that Charles Fillmore, co-founder of Unity Church, was in his nineties when he said, "I fairly sizzle with zeal and enthusiasm and spring forth with a mighty faith to do the things that ought to be done by me." Wow! That was enough to inspire me and start me sizzling.

I recognized some time ago that my enthusiasm for life is the secret ingredient I use when I am faced with difficult challenges (also known as opportunities for growth). The funny thing about this secret ingredient, and all the ingredients I am writing about, is that they are always available to you. Muster up a positive attitude filled with enthusiasm, and you are well armed to do battle against major challenges. Misery may love company, but so does enthusiasm. Whenever I see someone filled with enthusiasm about something he or she is doing, I am immediately invigorated and enthused about the things I am doing. Enthusiasm really is contagious.

I associate enthusiasm with keen interest and warm emotion. When you project enthusiasm, interest, and warmth, it is easier to get your message across, reach people you don't know, and touch people you do know. I think all manner of communication improves with enthusiasm. If you listen carefully to a news anchor on television or a broadcaster on radio, you'll notice that the he or she chooses to emphasize certain words or phrases in every sentence and maintain a lively tone of voice for every story, no matter how routine. Without enthusiasm, you come across as apathetic, as if you don't care a twig for what you're doing or saying.

Remember that waking up each morning is reason enough to be enthusiastic. It is your choice to be pessimistic or optimistic about the new day. Why not choose to be optimistic *and* enthusiastic?

Tomorrow morning when you wake up to start a new day, repeat the following words like you really mean them: "I am alive, awake, alert, and enthusiastic about life!" Whose life? Your life! Waking up is really the only reason you need to be enthusiastic. If you wake up, it's a great day!

Secret Ingredient: ENTHUSIASM
Like imagination, enthusiasm is part of the fun of doing anything that's worth doing. If you begin with this ingredient, you are sure to get off to a good start. Once you have folded it into the mix, keep mixing it up with enthusiasm.

FINAL WORDS:

Make a joyful noise.
— *Psalms: 100:1*

WORDS

You have to say what you are if you want to become what you wish to be.

— Robert Schuller

"WHO DO YOU THINK you are?" How many times has someone said that to you, questioning your reason for being the way you are?

Who are you? From your soul come the motivating desires and attitudes that are your core and your reason for being. The rest comes from your mind, which is your information bank. Herein lies the ability to learn, to remember, and to act based on what you know and, of course, on your creativity and imagination. Nearly everything we do independent of our bodies we do with our thoughts. Thoughts are silent and can only be communicated through words and actions. Though we rely on our senses for messages about the world around us, we also rely on words to describe the information we are getting from our senses. In the end, we have only words to express who we are to the world. In this way, words become a key ingredient in shaping our lives and giving us inner strength.

Since words are used to communicate the sacred, the profane, and everything in between, they can be smooth, powerful allies, and they can be sharp swords. The story of Cyrano de Bergerac illustrates the importance of words in the pursuit of romance.

Cyrano and his handsome friend Christian are both in love with Roxane. Lacking skill with words, Christian persuades Cyrano to provide the words that will win Roxane's heart. Sure enough, Roxane falls for the words Cyrano gives Christian and, because of them, she marries Christian. Only later does she discover whose love was in those words. Cyrano should have spoken up earlier and won Roxane's heart for himself.

The Bee Gees also paid homage to the everlasting power of words. In their song, "Words," the narrator begs his lady love to dedicate her words only to him and also to believe every word he says to her. "It's only words," he admits, but then again, words are all he has to win her heart.

Love songs were invented by marrying the magic of words to the magic of music. What sentimental heart can resist an arrow of words and music from Cupid's bow?

We've all heard that the pen can be mightier than the sword. Words can also be dull and fall on deaf ears. Unless we use them carefully and communicate clearly, words are of little value. Many of our difficulties in human relations are caused by improper or inadequate communication. When communication is unclear, we can fail to get our ideas across to other people or we can fail to hear what others are saying to us. Usually, misunderstandings result.

In childhood, we learned "sticks and stones can break your bones, but names can never harm you." I'm not sure they got that right. Bones and physical injuries can mend but the harm done by derogatory names and images can have a deep and lasting impact. Just ask an attorney about libel or defamation and the damage to a person's reputation that can be done by words. In the digital, Internet-connected world, images, too, can do a great deal of harm. When a Danish newspaper published an irreverent cartoon depicting the Prophet Mohammed as a terrorist, the Muslim world erupted in deadly and destructive riots. Is it necessary to draw such disrespectful images or use hateful language to underscore the freedom to express oneself?

When was the last time you got bent out of shape over words spoken carelessly to you? Angry words directed at you can hurt more and longer than a door slammed in your face. And have you ever been in a situation where you chose pointed words like an archer chooses arrows and sent them flying, knowing they would wound another person? It's easy to do. Next time you are tempted to fling outrageous words at another human being, remember how it feels. Then you will understand that our words can come back to haunt and hurt us, and often they do more damage to us personally than they do to anyone else.

Sugar dissolved in water cannot be retrieved, just as words, once spoken, cannot be taken back. Adding words of apology may ease the pain caused by the regretted words, but they can't erase it. Just as words spoken carelessly cause hurt, so do words that go unspoken. I have years of experience in saying the wrong things at the wrong time and not saying the right things at the right time. Having realized the importance of words in my life, I now make a conscious effort to be more open and sharing and to communicate accurately. I take the time to transmit my thoughts precisely. This adds value and meaning to my life and to the lives of others.

If you love someone, tell them and share the experience —
whenever the thought crosses your mind.

While I choose words carefully, there are some words I choose to
avoid, if possible. Among them are *minus words* like "if only," as in
"if only I had," and "but," as in "but I don't know if I can." "If
only" are words of regret like "could have" and "should have."
You didn't, so move on. "But" is a word of contradiction and
limitation, a deception and an excuse. Eliminating these words
and concepts from your vocabulary will enable you to
communicate more directly and truthfully.

Anyone who knows me will tell you that I never use the word
"try." I believe try is a non-word that prevents you from achieving
your goal. There is no action in try so you never succeed. In the
movie *The Empire Strikes Back*, Yoda says, "Do, or do not. There
is no try." Truer words were never spoken. Remove try from your
vocabulary today and see how much more you accomplish.

I also believe that the word "laughter" speaks volumes. Laughter
is the natural expression of a happy state of mind. It's a sure sign
of a healthy disposition, and it's good medicine, too. Seven days
without a hearty laugh makes one weak. Be very careful about
what words you use. Remember, we have only words to express
who we are to the world.

Secret Ingredient: WORDS
Choose your words carefully. If they are the right words at the
right time, use them liberally. If upon inspection, they appear to
be bruised, rotten, or otherwise spoiled, don't use them at all.

FINAL WORDS:

How often misused words generate misleading thoughts.
— Herbert Spencer

FAITH

For every web begun, God sends the thread.

HOW STRONG is your faith? It's a question that I often ask myself. When I look back at the road I've traveled, I see that faith has been a key ingredient of my inner strength even when I did not have a clear understanding of what faith was. Over the years, I have evolved a personal belief system based on many teachings and my own observations of the universe, yet I still strive to have a fuller understanding of what faith is. Even so, I know that faith plays an important role in thoughts and actions that enable me to overcome the many challenges I stumble into, over, and through.

The first inkling of faith I found in myself was a belief in the essential goodness of the universe. Even before I had faith in myself, I nurtured a positive outlook and a belief that things would work out. Later, I began to accept the notion that having faith was akin to having confidence in myself and what I was doing. Because faith in its fundamental form is a belief that isn't borne out by evidence or scientific proof, I began to see it as an affirmation of the universe and as a moment-to-moment perception that must constantly be renewed. How do you know that your well-laid plans will bear fruit? You don't; however, if your plan is sound and you do your best, you can have faith that the outcome will be positive.

Faith in God takes many forms. Not everyone worships in the same way. I note with satisfaction that our Sunday newspapers include information about dozens of places of worship, including churches, synagogues, and other religious gatherings. With or without religious doctrines, humans in every age and in every part of the globe have marveled at nature, at the miracle of birth, at the rotation of the seasons and the planets. It occurs to me that faith assures mortal human beings that the species Homo sapiens will be provided for and that babies will grow into children and children into adults, just as spiders weave spider webs, apple trees bear apples, and chickens lay eggs.

God has many names. Whatever name you give your God, some of us are not convinced that God exists in the same way that we are convinced that a chair exists. Even if some of us cannot be completely convinced of the existence of a higher power, faith is still possible because faith is something you do, not something you think. In fact, in some ways, the more you doubt, the more heroic your faith.

Ultimately, I think having faith is trusting that there is a divine plan that mankind cannot see. Having faith is accepting that the universe has plans for you. It's appreciating that the universe operates on a higher frequency than we do. Could it be that God is not finished making us yet?

In a practical sense, faith helps you replace negatives with positives. If your faith is strong enough, you can push negative thoughts from your mind and replace them all with positives. You can be a medium through which positive energy and positive thoughts flow. For me, I trust that the universe is in Divine Order even though I can't really explain it. Then, too, I can't explain electricity, but I trust the light will shine when I turn on the switch.

I am convinced that the way to live an inspiring life is to base all your decisions on a strong spiritual foundation. Any builder will tell you what you build is only as good as the foundation you build it on.

I use a combination of meditation and prayer to achieve a day-to-day understanding of my life. In her landmark book, *The Aquarian Conspiracy*, author Marilyn Ferguson calls this "direct knowing," a kind of intuitive knowledge. Without knowing the future, I know that the end result of every decision I make will not be exactly what I want, but it will be exactly what I need, and I can live with that. I don't know how intuitive the front man of the rock band the Rolling Stones is, but in a classic rock anthem, Mick Jagger sings, "You can't always get what you want, but if you try sometimes, you just might find you get what you need." I agree with the thought, if not with the word "try."

I say several prayers just about every day. Doing this fortifies me. It helps me maintain the strength to squeeze all the lemons of my life into a naturally sweet lemonade. One of the prayers is this: "Father, you lead me, and You know that which I do not know. And yet, You would not keep from me that which You would have me learn. And so I trust You to communicate to me all that You know for me."

Another is this: "Father I am peaceful; I am fearless. All things pass away. You never change. Patience obtains all things. I will want for nothing if I have You in my heart and soul. You alone are enough."

As I've mentioned, you may use other names to address God. It is not the name you use or the words you use. What counts about your prayer is the feeling you give it. Your faith is what you feel and what you feel is your faith.

Secret Ingredient: FAITH

Add this to everything you do, and you'll never be alone. What you fear does not exist. Fear is false evidence appearing to be real.

FINAL WORDS:

Fear knocked at the door. Faith opened the door and there was no one there.
— *Author Unknown*

CONCLUSION

NOW THAT YOU have all the secret ingredients for inner strength, what will you do with them? My hope is that you will use them to live a more positive life. Choose to enjoy every day. Choose to live a joyous, fun, and inspiring life. And please, remember these ingredients work if you work them. But don't take yourself too seriously. Be compassionate. Learn to laugh at yourself, forgive yourself, and move ahead.

ABOUT WALLY AMOS

Today, his name is a household word. Wally's most recent venture is Chip and Cookie, LLC, a retail store in Hawaii and online at www.chipandcookie.com, a business featuring two chocolate-chip cookie plush character dolls, Chip & Cookie, created by Christine Harris-Amos. In 1992, he formed Uncle Wally's Muffin Company, which produces a full line of muffins. As founder of Famous Amos Cookies in 1975, and the father of the gourmet chocolate-chip cookie industry, he has used his fame to support many educational causes. Wally was National Spokesman for Literacy Volunteers of America from 1979 until 2002, when they merged with Laubach Literacy Council to create ProLiteracy Worldwide. He now refers to himself as a literacy advocate whose primary focus is creating awareness of the values and benefits of reading aloud to children. He is also a board member of the National Center for Family Literacy and Communities in Schools.

Wally Amos has been the recipient of many honors and awards. He literally gave the shirt off his back and his battered Panama hat to the Smithsonian Institution's Warshaw Collection of Business Americana. He has been inducted into the Babson College Academy of Distinguished Entrepreneurs, and has received the Horatio Alger Award, The President's Award for Entrepreneurial Excellence, and The National Literacy Leadership Award.

In addition to this book, Wally has authored many other books, including his autobiography, *The Famous Amos Story: The Face That Launched a Thousand Chips*, *The Power of Self-Esteem*, and *Be Positive! Be Positive!*

Over the years, Wally Amos has acted in a number of network sitcoms and appeared on hundreds of interview shows, news programs, educational programs, and commercials. On the lecture circuit, he addresses audiences at corporations, industry associations, and universities with his inspiring "do it" philosophy. His fame is grounded in quality, substance, and a positive attitude.